CW00951995

Machiavelli's Lawn

The Great Writers' Garden Companion

Also by Mark Crick

Kafka's Soup: A Complete History of World Literature in 17 Recipes

Sartre's Sink: The Great Writers' Complete DIY Manual

Machiavelli's Lawn

The Great Writers' Garden Companion

Mark Crick

GRANTA

Granta Publications, 12 Addison Avenue, London W11 4QR

First published in Great Britain by Granta Books, 2011

A CIP catalogue record for this book
is available from the British Library.

1 3 5 7 9 10 8 6 4 2

ISBN 978 1 84708 134 6

Typeset by M Rules
Printed in Slovenia on behalf of Latitude Press

Contents

Introduction
with Niccolò Machiavelli

Those who strive to obtain the good graces of a reader are accustomed to come before him with things in which they see him take most delight, whence one often reads adventures and romances, histories of great men and women, the struggles of the oppressed, or of the many ways in which a reader may improve his well-being or success.

Desiring no alteration in your magnificent person nor to distract you with stories I consider unworthy of your countenance, I now present you with this small volume containing that which I hold most dear: knowledge of the habits and actions of great gardeners and plantsmen and women. I offer to you in this short form all that I have learnt over long years of study with so many troubles and so much expense.

Nor have I embellished this work with the allurements and adornments with which so many are accustomed to embellish works of horticulture. If in the imparting of this knowledge I have drawn as much on my studies of the great writers as on my long experience as a gardener I make no apology. The reputation of a gardener, like that of a writer, is made on his ability to uproot the unwanted and cut down the superfluous.

Introduction

Take, then, your Magnificence, this little gift. And if you take even some small pleasure from these tales of the parterre and the potager, you will see how I have with great and prolonged diligence sought only to win your favour and approval.

Planting a Hanging Basket
with Raymond Carver

Tools:
Hanging basket
Coir matting or liner
Compost
Slow release fertilizer
Plants
Water

That Saturday afternoon I was sitting on the sofa, reading the classifieds. You can learn a lot from reading the classifieds. Don't ask me what.

I was thinking about my mother. She'd written to say her TV was broke and she'd asked me to send her a little extra money that month. I'd agreed with Iris that I would call her that morning to tell her it was going to be difficult. "We've got troubles of our own," Iris said. "Why should we have to stake everyone?" she said. "What about your brother?" she said. "When did he last send any money?"

My brother hasn't got any money. She knows that. He stayed with us for a month back in the summer. He slept on the couch. He and Iris don't get along. Where he's staying now I don't even know.

"Your mother knows the plant closed," Iris says. "You told her, didn't you?"

Planting a Hanging Basket

"Sure I told her," I say. But my mother's old. She forgets. I waited until Iris was tidying in the kitchen before I made the call. Like she told me, I reminded my mother that I'd been terminated, that things were bad, but it didn't make any difference. My mother cried and said I was right to leave her to fend for herself. While she was talking I kept looking out the window, at the dead flowers in the hanging basket. In the end I said I'd send the money. Iris was listening as I made the call. She was still tidying the house but I heard her go quiet. When I hung up, she didn't say anything. After that there was a lot of noise from the bedroom and when she came back into the room where I was sitting on the sofa she was wearing her coat.

I saw she was there, but I didn't look up. I just carried on reading the classifieds, working out how little I could send to get my mother a new TV set.

I heard the door slam. Then her footsteps on the wooden porch. Ducking under that hanging basket and on past the shaggy lawn. The owner of the house we rented had put the basket up before we moved in. For the first few weeks the fuschias, the pansies, the lobelia had greeted us. Their bright colors hung over us every time we turned the key in the lock. But I forgot to water them. It was my job, Iris said. She couldn't reach. Anyway, I forgot. The colors began to fade and soon the basket was dead and

dry, rustling on windy days, nagging at me whenever I noticed.

I was sorry that I'd ignored Iris that morning, but I was waiting for her to leave so that I could plant up that old hanging basket again. I wanted to surprise her when she got back. After she'd let off steam at the mall. What could I say? I couldn't tell her what I was going to do, I'd told her too many times before what I was going to do and not done it. This time I thought I would use plants that didn't need so much care. The kind that could survive on a kind word now and then and little else. Heathers, ivy, maybe a cyclamen, I'd heard they thrived in dry conditions

I unhooked the hanging basket from the bracket beside the door and lifted it down. The plants had died so long ago, it was now just a basket of dust. There was a basket of dust hanging over the entrance to our house. Can you imagine.

I tipped the contents out onto the lawn. A cloud of dust flew up and a spider walked off under the porch. I took the basket to the faucet in the yard and washed it. It was made of wire coated with green plastic. In places the plastic had split and the wire had turned red with rust. Then I took a bag of compost and a tray of plants out of the car. I put them down on the step next to the basket. I lit a cigarette and sat on the step and read over the names of the plants. Someone had written the names out on little white sticks then stuck them

Raymond Carver

into the pots. "Pelargonium", "Petunia." On one of the tags,
". . . *amelloides variegata*", the name was so long that part of it
was hidden in the compost. Whether they were Greek or
Latin the words were all new to me. Luckily the sales assistant
at Plant Depot helped me to choose which ones would work
best in a basket.

From a round mat made of coir I cut the liner and pressed
it into the basket. At first the coir kept jumping up, so I made
some cuts in it with a pair of scissors. Straight cuts from the
edge towards the centre of the circle. Then I held it down
while I poured a little earth onto the coir and it stayed in
place. Around the basket's edge I made some holes in the
liner through which the flowers could hang. Then I mixed a
little slow release fertilizer into the compost and filled it level
with the holes, ready to put in the pelargoniums. I wrapped
their leaves in plastic so as not to damage them as I passed
them through the cuts I'd made and then added more
compost around their roots. It was important it was done
right.

I don't remember using any fertilizer the last time. The
plants were pretty much left to fend for themselves. The way
my mother feels.

I lit another cigarette and opened a beer. For once I was
in no hurry to get back to that sofa. I've spent a lot of time
on that sofa since the plant closed. Iris says I practically live

13

on that sofa. Then I put the lobelia around the edge, so that it would hang down and hide the rusty wire. I put in more compost around these too and left a space for the plant the clerk told me to put in the middle. He said it was a nice bushy plant with blue daisy-like flowers. I looked again at the tag marked ". . . *amelloides variegata*". *Felicia* it was called. Get that, Felicia. Iris had a little girl once called Felicia. It was before I knew her. I don't think she had her long, for a few hours I think she said. She doesn't even have a photograph.

The most important thing to remember with hanging baskets, the clerk said, was never to let the compost dry out. Once it dries out, he said, the plants aren't going to last long. He was right, too, that's what happened to the last one. I let the compost dry out. And then some. Iris says I should try drying out myself some time.

When the planting was done I hung the basket back on its bracket and went into the house to fetch water. The light was fading. My wife still wasn't home. While I waited for the can to fill up I looked about the kitchen. It took a while. There's some kind of problem with the water pressure, a bad valve, or something. Iris says if you want to take a bath on Thursday you'd better start drawing water on Monday. Anyway she's right, there's no water pressure. She'd really done a job on the place. It was tidy. Everything in its place, the way Iris likes

it. Except for an envelope lying on the kitchen table. I left the
can slowly filling under the faucet and I picked it up. My
name was on the envelope. No address, just my name, in
Iris's handwriting.

Growing Potatoes
with Bertolt Brecht

Armaments:
Spade
Fork

Provisions:
Seed potatoes

Position:
Trench

ACT ONE

A garden somewhere in northern Europe. A soldier with the rank of SERGEANT stands, head bowed, at the foot of a bed of freshly tilled earth. In his left hand he holds his cap, in his right there is some soil. In the ground at the top of the bed there is a cross. As he drops a little of the soil onto the ground a woman, pushing a wheelbarrow, enters stage right. She is dressed in eclectic style: wellington boots, hat decorated with ferns, around her neck a fox stole. The wheelbarrow is filled with compost on top of which are piled all manner of garden tools. Beside her, dressed in clothes more suited to a child of five or six years of age, walks a teenage BOY. On his head the BOY wears an upturned hanging basket from which fronds of fern and grass protrude. He is attached to

the handle of the wheelbarrow with a piece of gardening twine.
On his shoulder he carries a rake. When she sees the
SERGEANT, MOTHER COURAGE lets go of the handles and
makes the BOY kneel out of sight behind the wheelbarrow from
where he watches, the handle of his rake pointing upwards.
Wiping her hands on her apron, she views the soldier with
distrust. Finally she speaks.

MOTHER COURAGE. What do YOU want?

SERGEANT. (*Looking up from the ground. Placatory*) Mother
    Courage, that's no way to address an old friend and an
    officer of the King's army. I see your bereavement was a
    recent one. No name yet on the cross. My condolences.

MOTHER COURAGE. I'm reserving it for you. That would
    put a smile on my face.

SERGEANT. (*Looking at the earth in his palm*) I must
    compliment you on the quality of the grave. Full sun, good
    drainage, fertile soil, rich in organic matter. A pleasant
    spot indeed. Big man, was he?

MOTHER COURAGE. He was fifteen, and half starved. You
    ought to know.

SERGEANT. I only recruit them, what they make of army life
    is up to them. (*He sees MOTHER COURAGE and her son*
    staring first down at the ground and then up at him.)

MOTHER COURAGE. I brought him home from the

battlefield in this wheelbarrow. He didn't weigh much
more than a barrow of grass clippings.

SERGEANT. Well, you needn't look at me like that. I'm not in
recruitment any more, I'm in procurement. You know
what that means? The army's hungry, Mother Courage.
There's a war on, and war requires vegetables.

MOTHER COURAGE. The army's good at making
vegetables . . . of other people's children.

SERGEANT. Now, now, Mother Courage, let's not be like that.
Your sons brought glory to your name. (*The SERGEANT's
attention turns now to a second patch of dug earth.*)

MOTHER COURAGE. Glory's not much use for making a
soup. How's the Colonel? Eating well, is he?

SERGEANT. We're none of us eating well, Mother Courage.
(*He looks around.*) Eighteen-inch paths between the beds.
Beds no wider than five foot, paths on all sides. Would I
be right in thinking . . . This little plot has all the
hallmarks of a well-planned vegetable garden. Are those
potatoes over there?

MOTHER COURAGE. No, they're not. They're weeds.

SERGEANT. They don't look like weeds. My guess is this is
your main crop, Mother C. What are they? Cara? Désirée?
Pentland Squires? The boys love Pentland Squires. Too
much to hope for a few Pink Fir Apples for the chef's salad,
I suppose. What sort of weather have you been having?

MOTHER COURAGE. Shocking.

SERGEANT. Come, come now, in early September? Don't tell me you haven't had ninety to one hundred and forty days free of frost by now. More than enough for a healthy crop of spuds. Pests?

MOTHER COURAGE. Worst year ever. Cutworms, slugs, potato cyst, eelworms, blackleg and violet root rot. It's a battlefield.

SERGEANT. That won't bother the regimental cook, he makes a lovely dish of violet root rot. Men love it. I'll take 'em.

MOTHER COURAGE. (*Screaming*) Take my spuds? You might as well take the children, take us all. They're all we have to eat.

SERGEANT. Don't worry about feeding the children. The new recruiting officer will be along shortly, he'll be glad to take them off your hands.

MOTHER COURAGE. They're not ready.

SERGEANT. (*Looking now at MOTHER COURAGE's son peering over the wheelbarrow*) Not ready? Look at him: no father, an empty belly and shaking like a leaf. I never saw a lad more suited to army life.

MOTHER COURAGE. Not him, the potatoes.

SERGEANT. Oh, them, I'm not worried about them. I know you, Mother Courage. No one drills a crop like you do.

Drills dug three to six inches deep, spuds positioned fifteen inches apart, sprouts upward, am I right, Mother Courage? The stems well earthed-up to prevent any of your shallow crops from turning green in the sunlight, a light layer of straw to cover them on frosty nights. There's not a soul round here knows how to take care of their spuds like you. Pass me that fork. (*The two of them fight over the fork. The SERGEANT wins, pushing MOTHER COURAGE to the ground.*)

MOTHER COURAGE. (*Screaming*) You can't just dig them up. You need to cut the stems down first, then you leave the potatoes in the ground for another two weeks.

SERGEANT. Two weeks? What's the point of that? My men need feeding now.

MOTHER COURAGE. To harden the skins, you callous bastard. They'll be too tender, The shock of lifting them would be too much.

SERGEANT. The army? Wait? The army is hungry.

MOTHER COURAGE. The army's always hungry. And the army can never wait. Why does it have to keep picking my fruit to feed it? Oh, my poor boy that you took and never brought home to me. Why don't you just piss off and die for a change. (*She sings. The BOY, his head just peering over the edge of the wheelbarrow, takes up a trowel and begins beating time on a spade.*)

They mowed him down.
they peeled his skin,
they mashed his flesh
and then they dug him in.

Oh, the army
plants our boys in trenches,
fertilised with glory in the mud,
an early crop, that never quenches
the war's appetite for blood.

Boys who once were,
the apples of our eyes
are now a crop rotting in the ground,
unharvested though not forgotten,
fed and watered with politicians' lies.

They mowed him down,
they peeled his skin,
they mashed his flesh
and then they dug him in.

(*Singing mournfully now*)
I dug him out,
with a hoe and a prayer,
I kissed his cheek
but his cheek wasn't there.

SERGEANT. He keeps good time, that boy of yours. We need a new drummer boy. The last one had his arm taken off by a cannonball. The troops don't follow him like they used to. Wouldn't you like to be a little drummer boy? (*THE SERGEANT bends down towards the BOY and holds out a coin. As the BOY reaches to take it MOTHER COURAGE hits him across the knuckles with a trowel.*)

MOTHER COURAGE. He's not old enough.

SERGEANT. He looks old enough. How old are you, boy? Wouldn't you like to wear a coat of red and gold?

MOTHER COURAGE. Coat of what? Dead and cold you mean? Hang it on somebody else's child.

SERGEANT. Now, now, Mother Courage, let the boy speak for himself.

MOTHER COURAGE. He can't speak. I learnt my lesson after you took the last one. I never want any of my children to speak again.

SERGEANT. What do you mean?

MOTHER COURAGE. He knows what's best for him.

SERGEANT. All right, all right, the boy's none of my business, let's see what your potatoes have to say for themselves.

MOTHER COURAGE. Can't you even wait for a cloudy day? I wouldn't lift them in this light, they'll turn green in an hour.

SERGEANT. A dry, sunny day like this? Perfect conditions for harvesting potatoes. I'll soon have them out of the sun.

(Barking aloud the commands of a military drill, the SERGEANT uses the fork to present arms then, with a shout, as though he is making a bayonet charge, he begins driving the fork into the ground. Almost immediately a handful of potatoes is turned up.)

SERGEANT. Look at those beauties, Mother Courage. A few good thrusts from a soldier and Mother Earth soon spills up her guts. (MOTHER COURAGE has pulled her son close and together the two watch as the SERGEANT continues stabbing ferociously at the ground. When he stops the bed is devastated. All around him, potatoes lie on the surface of the ground. The SERGEANT wipes the sweat from his brow, and looks back now at the bed marked by the cross.) You wouldn't be hiding a crop there under the unknown soldier, would you, Mother C? (MOTHER COURAGE clings tighter to her son, her face defiant.) You'd be surprised at how many filthy peasants I've known cut all the foliage off a crop at the first sight of a soldier. What are you nurturing under here, Mother C? Nothing that a good prod with a garden fork won't uncover. (The SERGEANT now takes up the fork and repeats the drill. Then he begins digging the fork into the bed marked with the cross. MOTHER COURAGE wails. He uncovers something and falls to his knees in the mud and begins digging with his hands in the dirt.) What's this? Looks like parsnips . . . I knew it. You're a crafty old bitch, Mother C. Just for that I've changed my mind. I'm not even leaving you a handful of spuds for tonight's soup.

(The SERGEANT struggles now, pulling excitedly at the long white growths he has uncovered. As the bed is despoiled MOTHER COURAGE and her son grow increasingly troubled. When, after one last heave, the ground gives up its hold, the SERGEANT falls back, horrified, to see that he has been pulling on the skeletal fingers of a corpse. At the same time the BOY screams, a high, long, unbroken sound. Protruding from the ground we now see an arm. Clad in the filthy red and gold of a military dress coat, it is bent in such a way that it appears to be giving a salute. On seeing this mark of respect, the SERGEANT rises to his feet and, standing to attention, returns the salute. As he does so, the BOY resumes his drumming. This time the rhythm is that of Holst's 'Mars, Bringer of War'.)

Curtain

Dividing Bamboo
with Isabel Allende

Tools:
Fork
Saw
Spade
Faith

For two decades the treasure of Sergio de Flores had lain undisturbed. Its hiding place had been marked with a single cane of bamboo planted by the great bank robber himself. That cane had now become a clump whose ebony culms could be heard on windy days, whispering his name after dusk.

When Claveles came upon him one night, taking refuge in her garden, Sergio had begged her not to give him up to the police. And while she stared in wonder at his thick lips and heavy brow, he told her of the robbery he had carried out that very day and how, cornered by the police, he had buried its proceeds in the east bed of her modest garden. Before he left the following morning, he separated the cane from the potted bamboo on the terrace and planted it in the ground that covered his sunken treasure and swore he would love her till the end of his days. She, in turn, had sworn never to dig up the bed and never to ask him about its contents. And vowed to herself to water the single stem every day in honour of the mysterious lover whose return she awaited with a burning passion.

Their courtship was short. His proposal, made unexpectedly as Claveles helped him escape from the window of a ladies' convenience, was accepted with a heart overflowing with joy. The events of their wedding day were indicative of the relationship that was to follow. On hearing that a photographer from the local newspaper had arrived at the reception, Sergio declared himself overtaken by a sudden fever. While the bride, seated on a cloud of white organza, smiled stoically at the camera, her groom fled across the lawn on a stolen bicycle, pursued by a young man dressed in the uniform of the city telegraph office. She did not see the groom again until six days later, when he arrived early one morning having exchanged his Sunday best for a bunch of peonies, a false beard and a suit of green serge.

Supported by an unshakeable faith, Claveles grew accustomed to the sudden departures of her husband, persuading herself that his frequent absences and the impassioned partings that preceded them held a tragic romance that kept their love new and the passion of their youth evergreen. Once, in the spring of the fifth year of their marriage, her husband was gone for three months. Dispirited by his long absence, Claveles sought comfort in the now densely crowded patch of bamboo. With saw and

secateurs she cut away its dead and damaged culms, clearing
room for light and air, until only the youngest, most
intensely coloured canes remained. By the eightieth day of
their separation these tender cares had turned to obsession.
When finally he returned Sergio found his wife half crazed
with mourning. With ash-smeared cheeks, dressed in her
wedding gown dyed black, Claveles was standing in the
moonlit garden, humming to herself as she polished the
remaining canes until they shone like jet. From that day on,
frightened by such a spectacular display of grief, Sergio kept
his absences shorter.

Together the couple lived a frugal life. Claveles' modest
income, unsupplemented due to her spouse's reluctance to
take a job, soon found itself stretched by the demands of his
outlaw life. Whenever Claveles grew tired of their meagre
existence and questioned why they should deny themselves
the fruits of her husband's life of crime he laughed at her
simplicity. The police, he would say, were waiting for just
such an oversight. His success in avoiding prison lay, he
claimed, in his refusal to spend a single peso of his daringly
acquired fortune and in his readiness, at any moment, to
leave the comforts of his home for the open road. This he did
frequently. On feast days and festivals it was her husband's
custom to arrive late or leave early and he formed a habit of
fleeing the house before noon on Christmas Day, claiming

the police would call for him on just such a festival expecting to find him at his home.

These often unpredictable absences did nothing to diminish Claveles' unalterable devotion. When she begged him to take her with him his refusals were stern, his severity tempered by the passion of his goodbyes and his descriptions of a shining future in which she would wear dresses and jewels fit for a queen, and they would live every day together on a galleon moored in the rolling canopy of the rainforest.

Between them they invented a secret language of signs that would alert him if ever the police were to set a trap for his return. The hips left on a climbing rose to tell him that sharp shooters were lying in wait on the rooftop; runner beans trained into a cross of St Andrew as a sign that a patrol lay in the potting shed; the water lilies turned upside down on the surface of the pond, a signal that the captain and his guard were holding Claveles prisoner in the house. None of these scenarios ever came to pass but Claveles rejoiced in these and a hundred other subterfuges, revelling in the fantasy that each time her lover came to her he risked his life to share her bed.

In the last month of his life, Sergio de Flores succumbed to a fever of the brain. When, for the first time, Claveles saw her handsome bandit listen without alarm to the sound of steps approaching their door, she knew then that his sickness was grave. For twenty-eight days the fever raged, and while the bank robber gave voice to the ravings of his demented mind, and spoke of treasures lost and loved ones left behind, Claveles, blissfully, wiped the sweat from the muscled contours of his body. The period of his sickness was by far the longest time Claveles had spent in the company of her husband. And as she held a sponge soaked in honeyed water to his parched lips she gave thanks to God for the fever that kept him by her side, cherishing every moment spent enveloped in the sharp aroma of his sweat. Only when the affliction spread to his heart did her gratitude diminish and her prayers for his recovery begin in earnest. But by then it was too late. At its peak the fever grew so intense and Sergio's temperature so high that Claveles smelt the hair singe on her head as she lay against his burning cheek. When finally his temperature subsided it was not because the fever had broken; rather that it had consumed him, as a forest fire burns until there is no more to burn and de Flores, cradled in the blistered arms of his wife, breathed his last and died.

Half crazed with grief and remorse, Claveles took a spade and, as her husband's body lay cooling, she walked out into the garden. Unmindful any more of the promises she had made, or of the warnings she had been given, she made her way to the tall thicket of black canes, and there, like a fighter making a mark in the sand, she took the broad blade and drew a line in the ground.

Years of neglect had packed the soil about the bamboo as hard as granite so that breaking even its surface was a struggle. Stepping on and off the spade as she struggled to make headway she felt the sweat trickle down between her breasts, making her cotton blouse stick to her still elegant figure, but the blade did not budge.

So consumed was she by her battle with the earth, she did not notice the young passerby who had stopped to watch her work. Intrigued by the delicate woman balanced on the stationary blade like a trapeze artist on a wire, the young onlooker watched until finally the impatience of one who goes unnoticed prompted him to speak. "Can I help?" he asked.

Though the voice of the stranger was gentle, there was a familiarity to his features that at once unsettled her. Through long years spent listening to the cautions of her husband Claveles had grown secretive. Warily she watched him raise his foot to rest it on the fence. Then, ignoring his question, she looked back at the ground, ruefully surveying the minor cuts and scratches produced by her exertions with the spade. She looked back at the questioner and this time saw how tightly the fabric of his trouser hugged his thigh. His leg was heavy and the ground, as she had discovered, was very hard.

"I am trying to lift this bamboo. But the ground here is packed solid and I am so slight."

Requiring no more invitation, the chivalrous onlooker leapt the fence and, offering his hand as he bowed, waited for Claveles to step from the spade as though he were helping a countess from her carriage. Accepting his offer Claveles stepped from the spade and watched in awe as now, in the young man's hands, its unremitting blade began to cut through the earth like the hull of a boat through water.

Rejoicing in the unexpected opportunity to display his strength, the handsome digger stole surreptitious glances at the tearful gardener by his side, hoping for a sign of admiration and so beguiled by her tears that eventually he asked, "Does this plant mean something special?"

"My husband planted it."

"You're fortunate to have a gardener for a husband. My father has never gardened once in his life."

"It is the only thing he ever planted in this garden," she said and with her sleeve she wiped the tears from her cheeks and smiled. "I met him here, on this very spot. He was standing there where you are standing now. And I loved him from the first."

"Does he know you are digging it up?"

"My husband is dead."

She waited for him to speak, but the stranger only bowed

his head and resumed digging; only once, when a root resisted, did she hear the hoarse panting of his breath, sounding as though it came from far away, and her body began again to shake with silent weeping.

When the clump was nearly free she became anxious about uncovering the treasure whose secret she had kept for so many years, and she thanked him for his work and gestured him away. But the root ball, when she tried to lift it, was much heavier than she expected. Seeing her struggle the young man stepped forward again, and together the two of them began to lift the shallow rooted plant until, with a wrenching sound, it came free, like a city bristling with skyscrapers leaving in its wake a crater in which only dust could be seen. In vain Claveles ran her fingers over the earth searching for the lid of a strongbox, the decaying canvas of a bag of coin, and finding only dust.

"What is your name?" she said.

"Sergio." At his reply a shiver went down Claveles' spine.

"Sergio, the hole is not deep enough. Dig deeper. I will pay you for your trouble."

On her knees now, Claveles crouched over the deepening hole, her hands clutched together as if in prayer while the young man kept digging.

With each cut the hole grew deeper and the digger grew more concerned for the tragic creature, muttering strange incantations into the growing void. When the hole was nearly four feet deep, and as wide again, she told him to stop. Her arms wrapped about her slender body, her attention turned again to the clump of soil that held the knot of black canes. "Cut it in two. Cut the root ball in half."

When it became apparent that the cluster of roots had grown too dense to be cut easily with a spade, Claveles fetched a saw. She watched the hypnotic movement of his muscular arm as the newcomer knelt beside her and began to cut through the knot of roots that held together the tall canes of bamboo. When the clump was nearly divided he put down the saw and with only his hands began pulling apart the last of the soil, carefully trying to keep as many as possible of the young shoots intact. In that moment, thinking she saw a glimpse of something gold, the desperate widow clutched at the lump of earth, clawing and picking at the roots.

"Take care," said the good Samaritan, snatching the roots out of her reach. "If we are replanting we should keep as much earth as possible attached to the roots." But overcome with fear and impatience, Claveles, seeing not so much as a single peso fall from the dense mass of rhizomes, no longer cared.

"Cut again," she said. Soon the two clumps of bamboo had become four. Still not a grain of gold or silver could be seen. Again and again Claveles gave the order to cut until the garden was strewn with the black canes that lay about their feet like a morbid calligraphy, their message decipherable only to Claveles, who now began again to sob pitifully. "The doctors have taken the last of my money. My husband lies still on his deathbed and I have not a penny to pay for him to be buried."

"Your husband is not yet buried?" Sergio looked down at the hole he had dug. "Where is he, then?"

The question seemed to startle the bereaved woman, who suddenly leapt to her feet and, with hands black with earth, ran from the garden and into the house.

When finally the young man grew tired of waiting he followed her. When he found her she was slumped on the floor in the bedroom. Beside her on the bed, his face and body smeared with dark patches of earth left by the distraught hands of his kneeling wife, lay the body of Sergio de Flores. Claveles appeared calm now. Seeing the stranger pause respectfully in the doorway, her heart went out to the young man, who could not have expected such a scene to follow his act of kindness. His wide eyes filled with tears. Then with a shout the visitor ran forward, uttered the name of his father and fell sobbing across the body of the dead man.

Confused by the stranger's extraordinary outburst Claveles was at first slow to understand. Then she looked more closely at the young face, twisted in grief, and at the thick lips and heavy brow of her dead husband. Slowly a picture began to form. For the first time Claveles began to understand the nature of the half-life she had lived with Sergio de Flores, and the mystery of the half she did not know. And grief swept down on her in a new guise.

When the first shock of their shared grief had passed, the two survivors began to talk. The son told how, when his father had not returned home, inspired by a dream, his mother had sent him to look among the narrow streets and gardens for which Claveles' neighbourhood was well known. Together they remembered Sergio's wandering and invasive habits and the difficulties of containing this most expansive of characters.

Between them they carried the deceased to the hole left where the bamboo had once grown. There, with the dead man's knees touching his chin, they arranged the body in the position of the last rest. When his son remarked that there was scarcely a foot of space between his father's head and the surface of the ground his widow's answer was clear. "For a man like him it is enough," said Claveles. "He knows how to keep his head down."

After he had shovelled home the last of the soil the younger Sergio collected two of the black canes from the ground, still with part of the root ball attached. "Shouldn't we make a cross?" he said.

"I have a better idea," said Claveles and, taking one of the black rods from his hand, she made an ample hole in the freshly dug ground at the edge of the grave. Dousing it well with water, she planted the rod alongside the grave; then she planted another, and so on, until all of the canes had been used up and their dark stems rose up about the grave like the bars of a cage. Together then, the deceased's wife and child joined their hands in prayer, and standing before the dark bars of his prison, whose walls would continue to grow ever higher, the two mourners offered a prayer for the soul of Sergio de Flores, a divided man perhaps, but one capable of putting down roots almost anywhere.

On the Art of Mowing
with Niccolò Machiavelli

Instruments:
Scythe
Shears
Poison
Implacable resolution

All gardens consist of three basic habitats: the flower bed, the mixed border and the lawn laid to grass. Of these I say at once that there are more difficulties in preserving a lawn than in the upkeep of any other. The varied character and diversity of a flower bed demands a degree of freedom such that could not be tolerated in a lawn. This freedom is extended further still in the mixed border wherein a multitude of species are permitted to cohabit with a more or less self-regulating pattern. Such behaviour may well be compared with that in republics or in the farthest outposts of a ruler's dominion, in which, by virtue of their distance from the capital, subjects exist in a state of near anarchy. How different then is the lawn, the capital, so to speak, of a gardener's territory, his court even, in which his talent is put under the closest examination and where unrest and treachery do most to threaten his government.

Therefore I say that a lawn keeper, between the months of March and October, ought to have no other aim or thought, nor select anything else for his study, than the art of frequent mowing and its rules and discipline. Regular mowing not only punishes delinquent plants but also contains the ambitions of those grasses and weeds who through rapid advancement seek to obtain prominence amongst their fellows. In this way a wise gardener is able to ensure the vigour of his grasses without permitting them to grow so great in stature as to present a challenge to his authority.

Frequency of mowing alone does not make for good government. The severity of the cut will also decide the success or failure of a gardener's rule. The gardener who shows himself too clement and sets his scythe to cut above one and one half inches serves only to encourage the coarse grasses to swamp the finer. By the latter I refer to the bents, fescue and timothy, all loyal grasses recognised as worthy inhabitants of the ideal lawn and yet known to have been overrun on many occasions by the barbarian invader. If, on the contrary, a gardener seeks to give a show of strength and sets his scythe to cut shorter than one quarter of an inch, he risks weakening the grass; he places its roots in danger of starvation, and the natural impoverishment that is the consequence of starved roots disadvantages the lawn as a whole. Of all gardeners it is most difficult for the new gardener to avoid the imputation of cruelty. His dominion is so menaced by dangers of every sort: docks and sorrels;

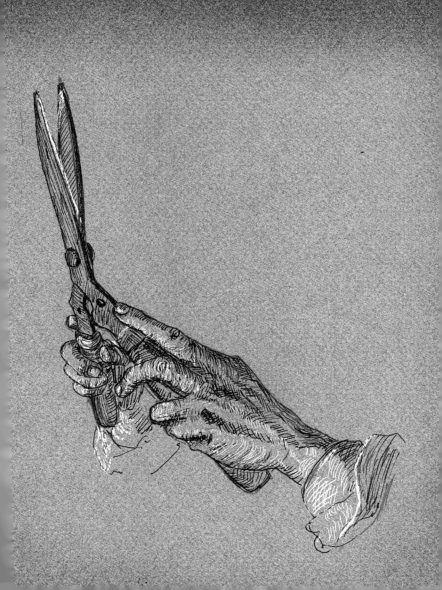

creeping buttercups; crowsfoot; the greater plantain and its
hoary relation, ribwort; starweed; clover; white lesser trefoil;
bird's foot trefoil; black medick; dandelion; cat's ear; daisies
and pearlwort, that if he is not possessed of genius or ability,
violence may be his only course.

The rule in mowing is indeed little and often. The Duke of
Milan, who cuts twice a week in summer when the grass is
growing vigorously, by applying a moderate force frequently,
finds his subjects are reassured and readily accept his rule.
The gardener who does otherwise, such as the Duke de
Sforza, who mowed less often but with greater severity, in
causing a sudden loss of such a large quantity of leaf in his
subjects, only encouraged the treacheries and invasion of the
outside mosses and weeds that were his downfall.

Moss in itself is of course not the primary cause of run-
down turf; it is rather a symptom of other weaknesses in a
gardener's mastery of his dominion. Underfeeding,
waterlogging and even failure to water during drought are all
possible causes of moss invasion and until these are tackled
the use of mercenaries such as moss killer will not return a
lawn to good health, but will remain a constant drain on the
resources of a ruler.

When dealing with threats and invasions of this sort the
rule is not little and often but to be cruel and excessive. There
are of course those, such as the Duke of Urbino, who preach

tolerance of moss and consider its bright colour and spongy texture merits worthy of inclusion in a lawn. I say that moss is the worst of treacheries, requiring a gardener to uproot it with the utmost severity.

Many gardeners are slow to react to the appearance of other apparently friendly threats such as daisies or pearlwort, both of which have shown themselves capable of spreading quickly and destroying large areas of grass in a relatively short period of time. The most effective check to their advance was demonstrated by Prince Cesare Borgia when in one single application of poison he successfully cleared the gardens of Castel Sant'Angelo of all the daisies in whom he saw an immediate threat to his authority. Nor do I doubt he would have hesitated to repeat this or any crueller treatment to be sure of eradicating other threats to his power.

The prince was fortunate in that daisies and mosses are not difficult to identify, but there are other less visible threats of which a gardener must beware if he is to govern well. Certain species of native and natural grasses, if inadequately suppressed when their land was originally taken from them, are distinctly undesirable. First among these are the coarse-leaved grasses: Yorkshire fog, cocksfoot, creeping soft grass and wall barley grass, all capable of forming unsightly clumps in closely mown turf, and the gardener that counts them among his citizens may never be sure that his lawn is entirely under his control.

A lawn that has been left for too long to live by its own rules ceases to be a lawn. It becomes instead a place of savagery, in which rivalling factions compete for territory, until the weak are overwhelmed by the strong. A gardener who finds himself in possession of such a territory, whether through fortune, inheritance or sloth, will certainly lose the respect of both and, unless he is willing to enter into a long campaign, has only one course of action before him. First he must drive out the troublemakers, by uprooting the lawn entirely, then, to avoid a recurrence of the uprising, the rebels and their descendants must be burnt and their ashes scattered on the ground. Only then will it be safe to repopulate his territory with more governable subjects. This he may do in two ways: either by seeding the cleared land or, if his fortune is sufficient, by the acquisition of rolls of turf. Neither path is straightforward; the sower of seed contends with the raids of birds and other thieves hungry for grain while the layer of turf must take pains to support the new settlers with provisions until such time as his colonists are established. In short there is nothing more difficult to take in hand, more perilous to conduct or more uncertain of its success than the laying of a new lawn.

May the troubles of all who embark on such an

undertaking serve as a warning to those gardeners who, neglecting the art of mowing, think more often of ease than of shears. The successful lawn keeper is never idle. He is master of his art and always undertakes his treatments before a problem arises. In this way troubles are kept at bay and his lawn remains an object of admiration to his neighbours.

Planting a Fruit Tree
with Henrik Ibsen

Props:
Spade
Compost
Hole

ACT I

*A garden. A grassy outcrop. About it a gloomy fjord landscape
shrouded in steady rain. At the top of the garden, half concealed
behind a small copse of trees, smoke rises from a chimney,
beneath it an attractive house with a conservatory. On the lawn
is JULIA, a woman in her early thirties elegantly dressed in
outdoor clothes. Her hat, pushed back off her head, hangs on her
back. Her wet hair sticks to her forehead. She is perspiring and
short of breath. In her hands she holds a spade. Centre stage, a
hole.*

*Beside the hole, in a pot there is an apple tree. With her free
hand JULIA removes her hat and hands it to HELDER, a man
in his late thirties, of sickly complexion. HELDER is sitting in a
bath chair; his right leg, extended straight in front of him, is
heavily strapped. He wears a dark overcoat, over his shoulders
and legs are rugs, and on his head he wears a hat with a wide
brim over which he is holding an umbrella. He is smoking a
cigar.*

Planting a Fruit Tree

JULIA. Is *this* deep enough? Can't we plant the tree now?

HELDER. Now what did I say, my little skylark? The hole
needs to be at least three times the size of the pot.
There you go again, my pet, always trying to take short
cuts.

JULIA. (*Pouting*) The hole looks quite deep enough to me.
Oh, Helder, it's quite a bore digging such a big hole for
such a tiny tree.

HELDER. When it comes to digging holes the rule is simple.
The bigger, the better. It also needs to be one and a half
times the depth of the root ball. Come on, my little
squirrel, one last effort and it will be done. Now you're
quite sure that the root ball has been given a good
soaking?

JULIA. Oh yes, Helder, I left it soaking this morning, at the
edge of the pond. When I went back the pot had become
so heavy I nearly fell in trying to get it out. I had to ask
Gunther to help me in the end.

HELDER. Dear old Gunther. It's good to have him back
round the place. The hole's looking good. Now if you pick
up that fork you can use it to scarify the sides.

JULIA. Whatify? Honestly, Helder, I've no idea what you're
talking about.

HELDER. Scarify. If we want our roots to be able to spread,
we don't want the earth at the edges of the hole to be

too tightly packed, do we? Use the fork to soften it up a bit. There's a good girl. Dear old Gunther seems to have taken quite a shine to our Oswald since he got back; he was carrying the boy on his shoulders when I passed them coming back from the village the other day. (*From off stage the sound of a child's voice shouting 'Charge!' HELDER and JULIA, who is now standing in the hole, both pause and look towards the sound. With joy on their faces the couple watch as their son, OSWALD, a rosy-cheeked young boy in a green sweater, runs past shouting with joy and exits stage right. JULIA's expression quickly changes to one of worry.*)

HELDER. (*Still looking towards OSWALD's exit*) How he does love to play with the gardener's son. It's hard to keep them apart these days. I suppose it's all right for now, but it won't do when he's older. Say, have you ever noticed, my little squirrel, how alike those two boys are?

JULIA. (*Uttering a cry, then, trying to disguise its cause, she quickly puts a finger in her mouth and sucks on an imaginary injury.*)

HELDER. What is it?

JULIA. (*Taking the finger from her mouth and examining it*) All boys their age are alike, Helder.

HELDER: Yes, I suppose you're right, my little skylark.

(*HELDER takes a puff on his cigar and watches JULIA*

struggling in the heavy soil.) Old Gunther certainly seems to be encouraging the friendship. Quite unlike his wife. (*Off stage, the occasional shout of boys at play is heard. JULIA looks at HELDER, then kneels down beside the hole and reaches in to pull out a handful of earth.*)

JULIA. (*Her voice appearing from the hole*) What do you mean?

HELDER. Don't you remember when Frau Gunther gave poor Oswald that terrible slap last summer? When she found him eating raspberries in the fruit patch. The boy's kept his distance from her ever since. She's not that nice even to you, I've noticed.

JULIA. (*Straining to reach into the hole and to remove the last of the loose soil*) She's nice enough. Tell me, Helder, your little squirrel is quite lost now, can I take the tree out of its pot yet?

HELDER. There you go again. Such an impatient little skylark. Always trying to rush to the fun part and never paying any mind to good preparation. You remember what happened when you insisted on decorating the Christmas tree last year before it was properly weighted in the pot?

JULIA. Yes, Helder, you're right. Sometimes your little skylark has no patience at all.

HELDER. You need to mix the soil you've taken out of the hole with all that lovely rich compost in the wheelbarrow there.

Imagine you're mixing the ingredients for a cake. (*Using the spade, JULIA lifts some of the compost onto the mound of soil on the ground and then stirs it with the garden fork.*)

JULIA. (*Playfully*) Aren't you glad, Helder, that your little Julia doesn't really make cakes like this? (*Looking up, she sees Helder is again looking towards the children at play. From her pocket she takes a paper bag and quickly pops a macaroon into her mouth. She tucks the bag out of sight then, pretending to be in a sulk . . .*) Helder, you're not watching what I'm doing. Very well, I'm going to take the tree out of its pot.

HELDER. You can, nearly, just as soon as you've put some of that cake mix into the bottom of the hole. That's it, a little more perhaps, let's make a nice little cushion for our apple tree to sit on. Now you can take the tree out of its pot. Lay it on its side first. Then you can pull the pot away from the tree . . . (*As JULIA crouches over the pot the bag of macaroons falls from her pocket.*) What's this? Has my little poppet been spending money again at the sweet shop? (*Guiltily JULIA shakes her head, then slides the pot away from the root ball and we see the earth, still holding together in the shape of the pot.*)

JULIA. Oh look, Helder. There at the base of the trunk. The tree has had a nasty misshapen ankle, just like you.

HELDER. Don't think you'll distract me from your little secrets so easily. Hand them over. (*HELDER holds out his*

hand. With a great show of mock guilt and shyness, JULIA
approaches HELDER and hands over the paper bag.)

JULIA. If your skylark promises not to do it again, could you
forgive her?

HELDER. (*Won over by JULIA's act*) I suppose I could. If she
kept her promise not to do it again.

(*JULIA kneels and takes one of the macaroons from the confiscated*
bag. With one hand she removes the cigar from HELDER's mouth
and with the other she places a macaroon between his lips.)

JULIA. (*Making eyes*) Could you forgive her anything? If she
promised not to do it again?

HELDER. Anything? . . . I'm not sure about anything.
(*Looking up at HELDER, JULIA begins to make little*
whining sounds like a puppy.) Well, I suppose I could.
(*Sterner*) If I thought she'd learnt her lesson . . . and could
keep her promise not to do it again. (*JULIA springs up to*
her feet and hugs HELDER. Then she returns to the tree by
the hole.) And that swelling at the base of the trunk, it's
not an injury, it's where the cultivar has been grafted onto
the rootstock. Oh, there's so much my pretty little
squirrel doesn't know, isn't there?

JULIA. Cultivars? Rootstocks? I'm sure I have no idea what
you're talking about.

HELDER. Most fruit trees are grown onto a rootstock, usually taken from some sturdy variety that knows how to take care of itself. As for the cultivar, well, that could be any variety chosen for the beauty of its flowers or the quality of its fruit. That's it, tease some of the roots out from the root ball so that they don't carry on growing around in a circle.

JULIA. (*Carefully pulling the roots out so as to keep as much soil as possible around them*) Isn't it wrong to grow one plant on the roots of another?

HELDER. Not at all. If the rootstock is a better provider of food and water, or better suited to the land in which the cultivar is to be grown, then why not? If giving a tree the best possible chance of success means doing it on roots that have proven themselves fittest for the job, then that's what we should do. You can put it in the hole now. Keep it nice and straight.

JULIA. What would Pastor Manders think?

HELDER. Exactly the same thing, I think. Why, at the vicarage he has a whole orchard grown on exactly the same principle. That's it, you can begin filling the hole now with your cake mix.

(*At first JULIA holds the tree straight, then as more soil is added it stands upright by itself, and she adds the rest of the soil and compost mix.*)

HELDER. Now tread the soil down with your foot to make sure the tree is properly anchored in the ground. (*Looking up*) I swear this rain is getting worse. It's good for the tree, but we'll have to get you in by the fire, my bedraggled little squirrel. Come along.

(*JULIA lays the spade across HELDER's lap. By now the wheels of the chair have sunk into the lawn and JULIA makes heavy work of pushing HELDER back in the direction of the house. The couple moves up stage, fading into the rain and mist. In the distance the silhouette of a man with a boy on his shoulders can just be made out. When JULIA sees it, she pauses and begins to adjust the rug on HELDER'S legs.*)

JULIA. I know you will forgive me, but before I go to the fire, Helder, I have something to tell you.

Curtain

Removing a Sucker

with Bret Easton Ellis

Tools:
Hunter wellington boots in classic green
Gold Leaf Tough Touch gloves
Sneeboer hoe
Felco Professional Model 7 secateurs

I'm wearing a four-button Sea Island cotton shirt in citrine
from Saks, moleskin trousers in Ohio green by Ralph Lauren
with a Mulberry belt in tan leather, when I step out onto the
roof garden of my apartment on the Upper West Side.
Panning over the mixed border the bright sap-green stem
catches my eye. It seems cleaner, more vibrant than its
neighbours, an emerald green diagonal nearly six feet long.

My fingers move now to my hip, and as my green Hunter
wellies step onto the buoyant sward of the artificial lawn, I
pull the Felco Professional Model 7 secateurs from their
holster. The Felco no. 7 is a superbly designed ergonomic
bypass secateur aimed at the professional. It has a rotating
handle that revolves on its axis, allowing the fingers to move
naturally, reducing the blisters and hand fatigue that can
accompany prolonged pruning. Its unique swivel action
requires up to thirty per cent less effort than conventional
models and offers maximum comfort. The swivelling handle
took some getting used to at first, but now I wonder how I

ever lived without it. Neither the cutting nor the anvil blades are riveted, so they are easy to replace and their narrow, pointed design allows for exceptionally close cutting. It's hard to appreciate all its benefits on the first cut, but believe me, this is the ultimate secateur and you'll want to savor its qualities over time.

How the fuck did this thing grow so big? So fast? Up close I count the number of leaves in each cluster . . . There are seven of them. Not five, but seven. They're paler, too, and the thorns are a different shape to those on the main plant. It's a parasite, a waster, a bum, panhandling life and energy away from the cultivar from whose rootstock it's sprung. It's a sucker.

In this garden alone there are so many parasites I can no longer keep count. Aphids, caterpillars, mealy bugs, red mite, whitefly, slugs, snails, mildew, mould, rust, scab, wilt, tulip fire, bud blast, canker and squirrel. Fucking squirrel. Bulb-eating, fruit-stealing, nut-burying fucking squirrel. All this in one tiny urban patch of green. The last year alone this garden has known more toxic liabilities than a fucking Wall Street bank.

I put the secateurs back into the holster. Cutting it back isn't going to work, to this kind of sucker that's just more stimulation to grow. Pretty soon I'll be overrun with the suckers. No, I am going to rip it off, with my bare hands.

Correction: I'm wearing Tough Touch gloves by Gold Leaf. After the manicure I had the yesterday I'm fairly confident

they'll keep out anything the garden might throw my way. I press down on the sucker's stem, watching as it springs back, vibrating, more elastic and flexible than the darker old wood of the cultivar. I trace along its length until I reach the spot where it disappears beneath the freshly tilled earth. One of those dumb fuck Mexicans poking around aimlessly with his hoe must have caused it. A small nick in the rootstock, that's all it takes, one little jab in the dark and next thing you know another sucker is born.

Holding the cherry-wood handle of a Sneeboer hand hoe I begin pulling earth away from the base of the plant, digging the last part with my hands until I have exposed the place where the sucker emerges from the rootstock. With my thumb and forefinger I take hold of one of its thorns and bend it back. When it snaps away from the stem it leaves behind a little ellipse-shaped wound of raw white flesh. It is pathetic how easily the sucker is stripped of its defences. I break off another and another. When I grow bored with breaking off the thorns I wrap both hands around the defenceless stem and squeezing tightly I wrench the sucker away from the root. There is a pop, then the sound of fibres tearing, epidermis, cortex, cambium splitting away from the root and finally, as the sucker comes away in my hands, taking with it any dormant buds that might still be lurking at its base, green-white sap splatters my face and arms and I fall back through the foliage onto the Canadian cedar decking. I look at the white sap dripping from the stump, spilling like semen onto the soil. Beside myself, I press my tongue into the open wound. At the taste of the bitter juice I begin biting on the end of the amputated stem, tearing off strips of skin, shoving it into my mouth, choking on the taste of chlorophyll and cellulose and I cast the mangled sucker onto the lawn where it lies like a green length of intestine while I, happy to be burying the last traces of one more fucking parasite, begin filling the earth back around the rootstock.

From an open door comes the sound of a television, the theme tune to *Wheel of Fortune*. My shirt stained with earth and sap, I stand up among the flowers to look over the fence for the source of the music. On the other side, a copy of this month's *Vanity Fair* by her side, is a hardbody, sunbathing. She's pretty, too. She's wearing a green bikini with sequinned bra and jewelled briefs from Max Mara and matching green sandals from Sergio Rossi. Seeing me, she moves her weight onto her elbow and with her free hand raises her Persol sunglasses. "What's that on your face?" she says. I remove the gloves. My face is wet and sticky with xylem and phloem, sap and slime stain my cheeks and smear the lenses of my Wayfarer sunglasses. Then, as she watches, with my fingers I take hold of the nearest rose, spreading its petals like the multiple lips of a too heavily made-up mouth, and sniff, inhaling its perfume. I slide my left hand down beneath its sepals and squeezing tightly I slash at its stem with the secateurs. The stem is half severed, I can feel the rose clinging on by a few stringy threads, struggling pointlessly. This time I place the blades around the stem and hissing I squeeze the hand grips close until with a soft crunch sound the rose comes away in my hand leaving its ragged stump pointing stupidly up in the sky. As I hold the severed bloom out over the fence, its petals shaking spasmodically, I can smell the scent of chlorophyll, I can feel the crushed wet stem cold on my hand.

"I want you to have this," I say. "Haven't I seen you at Daisy's?" She sits up on the teak and chrome lounger, sips from her Coke with a straw and I notice now how well endowed she is behind the sequins. She looks at the cut flower, my winning smile, the tanned muscles of my arm, the smeared black lenses of my Wayfarers. There's an awkward silence as I wipe the blades clean on top of the fence and then I say, "I've got a rather expensive bottle of Pouilly-Fuissé chilling in the house."

Finally she smiles. "I don't know Daisy," she says. "My name's Rosa."

Burying Bulbs in Autumn
with Sylvia Plath

Tools:
Bulbs
Trowel
Earth
Light
Darkness

I swallowed trying again to clear the bitter taste from my mouth then I tipped the bulbs from the bag and watched as their fat little bodies rolled around on the garden path. Bulbs with purple skin the texture of old oil paintings, pale anaemic bulbs trailing coarse tufts of root from their bodies, fat-bottomed bulbs covered from head to toe in maternity gowns that disintegrated at the touch, they all bounced and scuttled on the ground, for a moment like beetles startled to be caught in the light.

The dumpy little tubers, too dumb to think, then grew still, waiting to be put into the beds in which they would give birth to the offspring, now coiled like springs in their fat round bellies.

Daffodil or hyacinth? Tulip or snowdrop? I couldn't tell, so I separated the bulbs into groups according to their size. With the trowel I slit open the ground and cut a hole. The hole I made three times deeper than the depth of the largest of the bulbs and wide enough so that several of the little mothers could to be put together with a bulb or two's width between them. I looked at them, fat and passive, content to live their lives of endless reproduction, and I sank to my knees on the wet grass.

They disgusted me.

A clammy dampness soaked through my skirt and chilled my knees as one by one I laid the bulbs out on the dark mattress of earth. I arranged them in two rows at first, like beds in a hospital ward, until a piece of chalky stone, turned up by the trowel, appeared among the rows like a doctor making his rounds. Then I broke up the two lines and laid the helpless bulbs out at random, where they sat, waiting for the comforting weight of earth to close over them like a shadow.

I don't know how long I knelt there, growing more drowsy, looking at the bulbs and wondering which of their tight, translucent skins would split open first, and when it did what kind of plant would be first to emerge.

The watery November light began to fade. I saw the rectangle of yellow light falling on the lawn and thought of the children tucked up in bed. Like them I too grew sleepy. The fistful of fat bulb-like pills that I had shaken from the bottle and planted with so little care in my own body were already beginning to flower, their anaesthetising tendrils snaking over nerve and vein, and my head grew heavy.

Hurriedly now I folded the dark blanket of soil back over the plump little forms, swaddling them in the furry darkness for which they longed. I patted the earth until it lay still and flat, like water closing over a sinking stone and, fighting the urge to puke, I lay my cheek against its cool surface and closed my eyes.

Rousing myself, I lifted my face from the soil and hastily now I began to plant the remaining groups of smaller bulbs, in shallower holes, allowing as much space again between each sleeper. Once or twice, when I could not tell a bulb's top from its bottom, I laid it gently on its side hoping to spare mother and child the pain of an inverted birth.

When I had finished it was dark. Somewhere in the garden I could hear the rustling of the brown paper bag. Groggy now, on my hands and knees I searched for it, but it had gone, carried by the evening breeze to settle out of reach among the roses. I climbed to my feet and then dragged my unwilling limbs back into the house. In the kitchen I passed the note I had propped between the salt and pepper pots and I paused before the cellar door. Unsteadily I slipped off my shoes and barefoot I padded down the stairs into the darkness below. On a pile of old carpet, smelling of turpentine and damp earth, I lay down and felt the barricades of sleep rise up between me and the outside world.

Above me the dim bulb in the kitchen drew long furrows

of light between the floorboards, as though the tines of a rake were passing through the darkness overhead. I pulled the carpet over my face and the bright furrows disappeared from view. And like a penny dropped into a well, I sank deeper into the darkness, pressed down into the earth by unseen hands bedding me in for winter.

And I slept.

Weeding by Hand

with Émile Zola

Tools:
Trowel
Fork
Hoe
Hammer
Sickle

The last year of his life old Bonnemort had lain in his bed as the breath rattling through his rotten teeth grew shorter and more laboured and death patiently spread its tendrils through the old man's decaying body. For twelve full months the old miner's trowel and hoe had hung untouched on the back of the shed door, until the day that a fit of coughing came so violent that little streams of spittle, as black as pitch, ran down the sides of his mouth to gather like tar pits in the white hollows above his collar bone and Madame Bonnemort finally took down the key to her husband's shed and handed it to their lodger, Étienne.

Now the old man was dead and buried and it was Étienne who stood with the trowel in his calloused hand as he looked at the little parcel of land, so densely colonised that not one inch of earth could be seen through the labyrinthine thatch of weeds and grasses with which nature had reclaimed the ground as its own.

Weeding by Hand

Stems of fennel, long since turned to seed, rose up from this battlefield like the tattered banners of a vanquished army, outnumbered and overwhelmed by the hordes of thistle and dandelion that had breached old Bonnemort's defences. Nearby a few spindly leaves of rocket could be seen, struggling still to hold out beneath a blanket of bindweed and ivy over which ranks of bramble and chickweed advanced, smothering the life from the old man's crops as surely as the pit dust had smothered the air in his lungs.

Every day since the old man's death Étienne had come here from his shift at the pit, to trowel and to hoe, to fork and to dig, labouring to ease the burden of weeds that lay like the yoke of capitalism on this little patch of ground. At first the tools seemed strange to him, but he expected to get used to them and to become attuned to the rhythms and tasks of his new life above ground as he had grown used to the work of the mine in the tunnels below. It was in the trowel work that he suffered the most. Crawling on the baked ground he struggled to control the long blade in the heavy soil, frightened each time he worked to expose the long tap root of a dandelion or a dock that the root would break, knowing that where one weed had grown now there would be two, or three, each fragment capable of regenerating itself into a full grown plant as voracious as its parent for earth and light and water.

Moving about the beds on planks, Étienne did his best to compact the soil as little as possible, but however carefully he made his way through the unwanted vegetation, great clouds of seed and pollen flew up, carried on the air to settle wherever they fell and begin again the process of germination. Overhead seeds of sycamore, spinning earthwards, fell like poison rain, seeding the ground with thrusting young saplings that threatened, if unchecked, to become a forest. Demoralised, he watched this army of seedlings mobilising in such numbers that at times he imagined he could feel them germinating in the ground beneath him, readying themselves to burst up from the depths and overrun the earth.

In no time patches of dried blood drew tattoos on the backs of his hands, and welts of white flesh, raised by the nettles that whipped back and forth in front of his eyes, scarred his face. After long hours spent crawling on the hard ground, the flesh of his palms and knees grew raw and tender, forcing him to abandon the trowel and take up the garden fork. Then the sound of his clogs rang out, striking the tines of the fork like a bell as he set to work among the brambles. With an obstinate resistance the powerful flora clung to the earth, forcing him to dig deeper until the white roots of the plants lay bare in the broken ground. Only then, his back crying out under the strain, did he stoop to pull at their thorn-free fixings, so reluctant to give up this land that they had claimed as their own.

These plants that had crushed the life out of the once flourishing rows of lettuce and radish, courgette and cauliflower, seemed now to Étienne no less hard than the pitiless coal face on which he had seen so many men broken. The dull ache of hunger began to grip his empty belly but when he looked about him for something to eat his eyes were met only with the dense wall of undergrowth that rose up from the parched earth. Chewing on the bitter leaf of a dandelion, he saw that he was not alone. He saw that the earth itself was dying of starvation as it laboured to feed the million roots and rhizomes that pierced its flesh, and his heart sank. How greedy they all were, he thought. How pitilessly they clutched at the earth, sucking the goodness from every grain of soil, leaving nothing on which to raise the fragile plants and seedlings that he hoped might one day feed him.

From time to time neighbours and colleagues from the pit called by, to watch him work or to give advice. Some came just to make fun of his efforts. "That's the way," encouraged Harel, the school teacher. "Do your weeding while the weather's hot and dry; it makes the weeds shrivel faster and will give them less chance of clinging on."

Even la Levaque, the barmaid, eyeing him mischievously

as her breasts hung over the fence, had a word of advice for him. "The old man has done you no favours. Look at those dandelion clocks ready to drop. Haven't you heard, 'One year seed, seven years weed'? I can think of better things you could be doing with your time." Her coarse laughter echoed off the side of the old shed, making her breasts shake like dumplings boiling in a pot. But Étienne had no time.

"You're wasting your life," said Souvarine, the anarchist. "Look at the pollen rising. Every disturbance just increases your servitude. I expected better of you. Why don't you burn the lot?" But Étienne had not yet the stomach for revolution, nor did he share Souvarine's conviction that all plants are equal. He believed still that by peaceful means the good plants could be freed from the tyranny of the bad.

When he grew tired of their advice and could stand no more the glaring heat of the sun, the gardener withdrew into the shade of old Bonnemort's shed. Already Étienne had grown tired of the tyranny he had found on the allotment, where his new masters demanded even more of him than those in the mine. Sick with fatigue, he looked about him at the squalor of the old man's cabin. Baskets of tools and twine kept company with piles of terracotta pots; string bags filled with withered bulbs hung over seed trays labelled lettuce, spinach, green beans; seedlings all long past watering now lay dead and dried, like specimens in an apothecary's shop. On a shelf littered with the debris of the old gardener's life, a near-empty jar of sunflower seed caught his eye. Greedily he filled his mouth with its contents. Étienne then began poking among the dusty cans and bottles that crowded the shelves above, reading the labels written shakily in the old man's hand: coffee, sugar, weed killer, tomato feed, fertiliser. His hunger quelled by the excitement of these discoveries, the exhausted gardener began to dream. Was it possible that one of these containers held the secret of the succulent cabbages with which old Ma Bonnemort made her choucroutes and coleslaws? Could escape from the back-breaking cycle of labour be waiting at the bottom of a bottle?

For the first time he saw that the enemy was not the bosses, nor the mine owners and stockholders with their constant pursuit of profit, nor the citizens and their demand for lower prices, but nature herself; the nature that drove men to relive the sorrows of their fathers, the tragic marrow that lived in the bone. Numb with fatigue, the words of Souvarine echoing in his head, he felt sick at heart at the thought of beginning to weed again; it was too unfair, too hard. His human pride rebelled at the idea of becoming a slave to this patch of ground and he made up his mind. What was needed now was something cataclysmic. The anarchist had been right; a gardener must be prepared to wipe out everything and begin anew. Étienne looked again at the shelves of weed killers, uncertain of which to use. Weed killers that were to be painted onto the leaves of unwanted plants; weed killers that were to be soaked into the soil; selective weed killers that targeted only certain species. Looking at the contents of the cans one white powder looked much like another. Finally he made his decision. He would use them all.

Rapidly now, he began to combine the contents of all the jars and canisters into one lethal mixture, a fatal cocktail that was intended to wipe out tyranny and oppression once and for all. So impatient for his liberation was he that Étienne did not even notice that one of the cans held not weed killer, but sugar, the same sugar that old man Bonnemort had used to sweeten his coffee.

The sun climbed higher, beating down with increasing force on the little tin roof until the heat in the cabin had grown unbearable. Drowsily Étienne added the last of the ingredients to the deadly cocktail and crammed a lid onto the can. Then, gasping for air, his eyelids trembling in the glare of the sun, he staggered from the cabin. Dragging his heavy feet through the undergrowth, the exhausted gardener surrendered to the snares of bindweed and ivy and allowed himself to be pulled down into the tall grasses. He lay there and thought again of the old man until, overcome by the sun, under the swaying heads of creeping thistle, among the couch grass and horsetail, he dozed off.

When Étienne awoke the sun had passed its zenith. Groggily he sat up. His back was wet through, soaked with sweat and the bitter emanations of the leaves crushed beneath him, making his skin itch and burn. Insects buzzed about his ears. Through the nodding spires of buddleia only the roof of old Bonnemort's shed was visible. Patched with salvaged sheets of tin, it seemed to glow as though it had just been forged, the whole resembling nothing more than a miner's billycan simmering slowly in the heat of the sun. Bleary-eyed, parched with thirst, Étienne took up his trowel and headed back to the little cabin in which he had earlier mixed the potion that was to put an end to his labours. As he put his foot on the first step he noticed that the buzzing of the insects had suddenly stopped.

Etienne was on the top step when the door of old Bonnemort's cabin came off its hinges. Narrowly the door missed him, but the ball of flame that swept from the cabin enveloped him completely, instantly drying the sweat from his soaked clothes and burning the hair from his face and head. Thrown high by the force of the explosion, Étienne's limp body landed back in the vegetable patch, crushing the last surviving stems of rocket and parsley, and knocking the wind from his inflamed lungs with such severity that it was some moments before he could breathe again. When finally, his body shuddering back into life, he was able to suck in the

hot air through his scorched lips, his nostrils were filled with
the scent of his own burnt flesh. The trowel, knocked from
his hand, was flung from one end of the allotment to the
other and remained where it landed, in a clump of stinging
nettles that covered what had once been an onion patch. Of
the unwanted plants, a few had their leaves scorched by the
explosion, but Étienne's body had taken most of the blast and
the majority felt only a gust of hot air carrying their seed
higher and farther than before. The few weeds that were
burnt soon grew back. Etienne's hair, however, did not; not on
his head nor on his chin. His scarred and sensitive skin, he
found, was happiest in the darkness, and when his injuries
were healed it was to the darkness that he returned, resuming
his work in the mine. For the rest of his life the miner never
forgot his experiences on the allotment and if ever any of his
colleagues were heard to complain about the conditions
underground, Étienne's white face could be seen laughing in
the shadows. "Count your blessings," was his cry. "Cut coal
doesn't grow back in a season."

Caring for Heather
with Alan Bennett

Tools:
Secateurs
Acidic soil
Good drainage

Heather began her career in the window box of number 23
The Avenue, Morecambe, Lancashire. Although much was
made of her Scottish ancestry, number 23 was, in fact, the
closest she came to travelling north of the border, having been
raised from seed in the Wyevale nursery just off the A26
outside Cleethorpes. A window box is perhaps not the most
promising of beginnings for a plant, but nevertheless it was
one that introduced her early in life to the rigours of playing
front of house and kept her from the more sedentary
pleasures of providing ground cover in the mixed border for
the rest of her career.

As chance would have it, the owner of number 23, Mr
Crofton, still living with his Scottish mother though he must
have been well into his fifties even then, was the head
gardener for the local council and as such was also
responsible for the plant display that faced on to the
seafront's crowning glory, the Variety Theatre. Well it
happened that late one evening, the star of the show, leaving
the theatre after playing a near empty house and one too

many drinks in his dressing room, fell vomiting into the ornamental bed. Though the name of the actor escapes me, I still recall how, with unanimous verdict, the ladies at the bus stop agreed he was "a disgusting pig", a term coined first by my mam as she listened to the story told by Mr Crofton's mother, with whom we were waiting for the 96 bus.

Having been diagnosed as polluted beyond the realms of decency, the injured plants were removed, and Mr Crofton found himself, at short notice, in need of a performer who could cope with the now acidic soil and could also be counted on to suppress the weeds that will naturally fill any vacancy in a flower bed. Heather was at hand and a career was launched. She was still playing the seafront in various roles almost a decade later. Heather had a glorious season in 2005 when, in what must have been her busiest year ever, she appeared in no fewer than five displays, including a floral tribute to soldiers serving overseas, a fund-raising parterre for the RNLI and a final show-stopping appearance in the town's floral clock. Mr Crofton, still the borough's plantsman-in-chief, had cast Heather in a small supporting role for which, after considerable coaching and pruning, she was to represent the numeral 2 in what was to be the centrepiece of Morecambe's floral attractions that year. His ailing mother now suffering from dementia, Mr Crofton had left the maintenance of the clock to his young assistant and he, more used to dealing

with the softer foliage of pansies and pelargoniums, had overlooked the mid-spring prune to which Heather was so partial, and although this required no more than a quick flourish of the shears to remove Heather's flowers as soon as they died back, a sort of horticultural shampoo and set, it also served to prevent her growth becoming too leggy. As a result, within a month, at ten minutes past four on a Thursday afternoon, the clock's minute hand became entrapped in Heather's woodier growth. The resulting late start to the entertainments on the bandstand and the failure of a group of elderly French tourists to rejoin their coach on time, not to mention the consequent missed ferry, was newsworthy enough to make the local papers and within a week Heather found herself removed from the display in what must have been humiliating circumstances.

Insult was added to injury when, in his haste to cut her free, Mr Crofton's well-meaning junior inadvertently cut into Heather's old wood, leaving an unsightly brown patch from which she never flowered again. Thus disfigured she was put into storage, in a grow bag of ericaceous compost at the municipal nursery. It must have seemed to Heather that her career was over; until the following spring, when Mr Crofton, finding himself short of a gift on Mother's Day, had Heather potted up. Then, with a tartan bow tied neatly around her container, he drove her over to the nursing home in

Alan Bennett

neighbouring Heyshel. After a distressing twenty minutes being mistaken for his ninety-three-year-old mother's chiropodist, Mr Crofton left Heather balanced on top of the television set where she cut a lonely figure in this, the last stage of her career, as a rather unkempt and misshapen figure 2. And when later the increasingly confused Mrs Crofton began asking staff if it was her second birthday, it was thought best to remove Heather to the communal lounge. And so, in the twilight of her career, Heather found herself topping the bill on the window sill in the south-facing lounge of the Elmbourne nursing home.

Heather's real name was *Erica cinerea*, a name she found somewhat too exotic for her Lancashire public. She was not one for flashy display. Long before the current trend for banana trees and exotic grasses Heather had been a favourite in the rockeries that were so popular in her youth, her love of direct sun and tolerance of drought being just two of the qualities that made her so popular. So it was no surprise to me that she approached this last engagement with such professionalism, seeing no shame in the ordinariness of this final playhouse, nor in the drowsiness of this, her last audience, in whose watery gaze she might have glimpsed not just admiration, but also affection, the residents mistaking Heather's unruly mop on more than one occasion for a long-lost pet or rarely seen grandchild peering in at the window.

It was with no little sadness that I saw Heather for the last time while visiting my own mother in Elmbourne Rest Home just a few weeks before Heather passed away. By then Heather had lost the pink lilac colouring on which her reputation had been made, most of her flowers having long since dropped, and I imagine that many of her fans would have had great difficulty in recognising her as the young lass that had been such a hit in those early days on Morecambe seafront.

Knowing she loved to be in the sun, one of the staff had positioned her above a radiator, on a window sill so hot on sunny days that you could have boiled an egg on it. That wouldn't have bothered Heather so much as the lack of fresh air to which she had always been partial. And though Heather liked a drink, one of her many merits as a house plant was that she never minded being passed over by the watering can, a trait that must have caused her no end of suffering during the summer season at Morecambe, where rain topped the bill as often, if not more so, than sun. What finished her off in the end was too much water. When it came to plant care the approach at Elmbourne could best be described as feast or famine, and when one of the younger members of staff, noticing Heather's compost had dried out, stood her to soak stem-deep in a Tupperware salad bowl, the end was nigh. Hardly the ideal conditions for a plant of her temperament.

By the time I reached her it was too late. There were bluish-black stains on her branches, and beneath the voluminous skirts of her foliage ominous patches of decay were beginning to spread up the base of her stem.

She had succumbed to what gardeners describe as chlorotic leaf and root rot, old age being an unacceptable diagnosis in these politically correct times. But ten years is a pretty good innings for a shrub of her sort. Before I left, the manager of the home remarked on what an undemanding resident Heather had been. "We've had ornaments here that have needed more attention than that Heather. Wherever we put her she made the best of it," he said, unintentionally summing up the attitude of many an institution towards its older residents, not dissimilar to that of a lost property office towards forgotten parcels.

In the end there was a strange symmetry to a career that had its beginning on one side of a window pane coming to its end on the other, and a more fitting place for the curtain to come down, than on a window sill, I can't imagine.

Erica cinerea, 1996–2006

Propagating from a Vine
with Mary Shelley

Ingredients:
Cuttings compost
Fungicide
Vine or climber

It was a stormy night in August when I put down my travelling case and stepped again into the humid gloom of the potting shed. There, as the rain pattered dismally against the panes overhead, amid the scent of wet loam and cedar I first beheld the accomplishment of my toil.

How shall I describe the wretched creeper whose propagation ought to have been the crowning glory of so many infinite pains and cares? Animated by a convulsive motion, the strange Nepalese vine had grown with an ardour unimaginable, so that now its coils appeared to have overwhelmed every surface and upright of the humble outhouse in which for so long and with so little success my profane fingers had disturbed the secrets of the bindweed and the honeysuckle. Proof positive that I had finally succeeded in discovering the cause of propagation, nay more, I had become capable of bestowing animation upon a lifeless cutting. No father could claim more delight and rapture than I on first seeing his creation, nor understand more fully how my rapture turned to loathing, when by the glimmer of the half extinguished candle, I perceived the extraordinary sight (sight tremendous and abhorred) that greeted my arrival. What ought to have been my Adam had become rather my fallen angel, fallen with a vengeance, starving its neighbours of light and moisture, of air and space, strangling its brethren one by one, until alone the serpentine and unnatural vine held dominion over the potting shed.

How I came to make this breakthrough I will tell you. Learn from me how dangerous is the propagation of the unknown, how unhappy the gardener whose search for glory takes him beyond the borders set by nature.

In the pursuit of my studies it was my habit to spend long hours rooting in the compost heaps of my neighbourhood, seeking amongst death and decay the answer to the mysteries of plant propagation. Here I beheld the corruption of decay succeed to the shining surface of the leaf, here I learnt how quickly the blindworm takes possession of the petal of blossom and bloom and here too I saw with what distasteful haste mould inherited the rosehip and the cucumber. From such pits of putrefaction I salvaged the lumps of green flesh with which I would return to my potting shed, where, confident in the ultimate success of my undertaking, I planted them, sheltered from the scorching of the sun, nourished by the primordial peat.

As summer came on, the steaming heaps from which I drew my grotesque specimens became increasingly overwhelmed with grass clippings, swamping all else in a green slime that

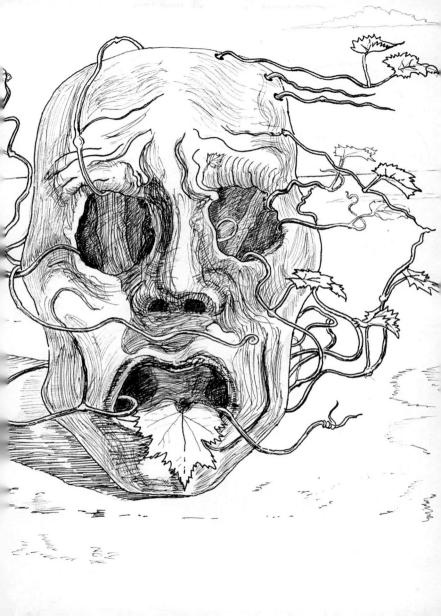

accelerated the process of decay, until for my specimens I came to depend on those brought to my door by students and colleagues familiar with the purpose of my studies.

Among these callers there came one night a dark-skinned man, his head covered and dressed after the manner of the hillsmen of the Himalayas. In his hands he held a length of vine, a piece of cord, I might have thought, in the hands of an assassin, were it not for the leafy couplets which interrupted its length. The cutting had most likely been taken earlier that evening, stolen, I didn't doubt, from the garden of his employer. I paid the fellow what he asked, and took the cutting directly to my laboratory, or potting shed as you might call it.

Seeing the stem was in excellent condition, I was moved to attempt for one last time an experiment I had tried earlier that year without success. I first removed the leaves from a length of vine and then, with the aid of a sharp blade, wounded the underside of the stem, scraping the epidermis with the edge of a knife so as to expose the watery green core. I then placed the injured limb in a trench no wider or deeper than a man's finger, covered it with earth and generously humidified the area with a fungicide of my own preparation.

The hour was late and since it was to be my last night at the house for some time I closed the door of my laboratory and retired to prepare my bags for the following day, when I was to make my way south to spend a month hiking the

Alpine pastures with my friend Henry Clerval. How I wish I had not taken up Henry's invitation, rejoicing in the salubrious Alpine air, oblivious to the monster taking shape in my own home amongst the unhallowed damps of the cold frame and the cloche. Now, nearly five weeks later, the demonic creeper to which I had so miserably given life had grown too vast to submit longer to the will of its creator.

While this vegetable devil destroyed the hopes of all its neighbours, still it could not satisfy its own desires, forever ardent and craving. Before me now, in the faint moonlight that broke through the dark and comfortless sky, I saw its blind buds, reaching even unto me, their creator, beckoning me closer, urging me to surrender myself into the life-sapping grip of a thousand tendrils. Where for so long I had pursued nature into her hiding places, now she pursued me, inviting me to find oblivion in its deadly caress and in so doing purge myself of self-loathing and guilt. Overcome by my own sin, the hubris of the gardener who in seeking glory fails to pay homage to the one true Creator, I yielded. And with a cry that set the panes of the greenhouse atremble, I threw myself into its waiting coils, ready for its crushing grip to strip the life from my lungs.

Repotting a House Plant
with Martin Amis

Horticultural aids:
Plant pot
Compost
Drainage material
Water – still or sparkling

You'll probably guess, before even my composted memory can retrace the events, that this is the story of a gardener, a suburban sward cutter, a Home Counties fuschia fancier, who finds himself far from home and in search of thrills. It's also the story of a prisoner, or a hostage at least, and a liberation. But however far you may take the gardener out of suburbia, you won't take suburbia out of the gardener.

My body is a dictionary. A dictionary of pain. From my arse to my zygotic nerve it hurts. It hurts a lot. There are earth stains on my shirt, on the bed. Rinds of dirt press insistently under my fingernails as though I've spent the night clawing my way free of a premature burial. God, I hate mornings, the endless succession of questions posed by my ageing body, that endless succession of surprises and pain as memory begins to taunt me and the first messages begin coming in from witnesses of the night before, checking to see if I am still alive.

My mouth is like a swarm of bees that only smoke will

calm. I take a packet of Downhill from the bedside table and light the first of the day. On the match fold, beneath the silhouette of a woman leaning provocatively against a palm tree, the legend Palms Lounge, its thermographed lettering straining against the confines of the flat surface, provides memory with her first opening and she hits me with a darting left jab to my paper-thin temple. The blow has shaken me. I'm a little unsteady on my feet as I stand, tightening the belt of my robe across the boulder of my gut, to call down to the desk for coffee. "For one or two?" says the desk clerk knowingly.

"For six," I say. "On second thoughts send me all you've got."

A rangy bellboy with an Adam's apple like a three-pound tumour puts down the tray of coffee. I watch his sleepy eyes widen in surprise at the sight of my loamy digits dismissing him with a tip. As I pour the first of the peat-brown liquid into the cup, memory strikes again. A combination this time. Left to the ribs. Right to the head and then a left to the gut. When I pick my crumpled jacket from the floor I can feel the heavy bulk pulling it out of shape. The rubberised grip is sticky in my hand as I lift the heavy instrument from the pocket and lay it on the table. And now, seeing my guard drop, memory unleashes a powerful right. My head snaps back, my gum shield flies from my loosening teeth and I fall

to the canvas. Fight over. I look up. From the table top the stainless blade of a garden trowel glints painfully in the morning light. It's all coming back to me. I won't be going back to Palms Lounge in a hurry, that's for sure.

While the first pint of coffee osmoses into my bloodstream and the compost of coffee grounds sits steaming at the bottom of my cup, I light another Downhill and begin running over the events of the day before. The contract signed, drinks, lunch, more drinks. The taxi to Palms Lounge. My colleagues whooping when the hostess greets me by name. Don't mock. I had a month to spend on my own in this city, I'd already spent an evening deadheading the rosebush outside my hotel. Twice I'd stayed late at the office to replant the necropolitan window boxes that blighted the views from every window. Gardening opportunities being limited after dark, what else was I going to do?

Located on the eastern fringe of the financial district, the Palms Lounge is a gentlemen's club. Like most gentlemen's clubs it doesn't see many gentlemen. Beered-up lawyers and rat-arsed accountants looking for low-rent nights to escape their high-rent lives are the backbone of the club's clientele. The lounge itself is a cramped basement in which everything that is not painted black is brown. Miles of exposed trunking and pipework zigzag back and forth across the walls and ceiling, carrying services no doubt to the fluorescent green office block that stands on the site above ground. Within their labyrinthine growth, the club's faux-leather furniture is clustered around a tiny stage like fat beetles in the gloom, on whose easy-wipe surfaces the patrons of the club gather, happy to take part in the club's fucked-up parlour games for pissed-up priapists.

After four weeks of coming to this place, four weeks of leering over Tilly Palmer's silicon valleys, four weeks of watching Hedda Foremen's irrepressible thighs threatening to burst the banks of their stocking tops, I'd begun to develop a healthy contempt for the scummy clientele who frequent this gloomy burrow. Not because of their shabby treatment of the syphilitic sirens bending over backwards to show them a good time, but because of their abject failure to acknowledge the plight of the pot-bound palms that sit dying on every table of this C-list flesh pot and meatery. I pick up the example in front of me and show it to my colleague, Stock Byers. Having outgrown their diminutive domain, its centipede-like roots protruded from the bottom of the pot, venturing forth presumably in search of channels of grime in which to feed. "Look at that, it's a fucking disgrace. Whoever's in charge of these ought to be sacked."

"They're sagging a bit, sure, but man, look at her move. I

wouldn't say no." Stock wasn't looking at the plant. His eyes were fixed instead on the gyrations of dancer number six, the concentric motion of her surgical augmentations apparently holding his sodden brain in a state of deep hypnosis. I pressed my thumb into the compost. Beneath the granite-like crust that had formed on its surface the potting material was dry and spent.

"There's no nutrients left in here, this thing needs repotting."

I raised my hand. Within seconds a shop-soiled hostess had stacked her pencil-thin thighs across my knees. "Dance for you, Mr Gardner?" she said, placing, with jejune charm, a slender hand against the inside of my thigh.

"No. Fetch me some water." Disappointment flashed across her face, but her response was automatic.

"Sparkling or still?"

"Do you think this thing gives a fuck?" I held the plant up to her face. "Two bottles of it. And bring me an ice bucket, *no ice*, and a corkscrew."

While I waited for the return of my sulky water carrier I watched Stock. Like two sunflowers tracking the approaching sun, his wide eyes followed Tilly's transit. Gripping the arms of his chair, he was craning forwards, his every feature beseeching the hot flesh upon the stage to engulf him in its sordid warmth. When his call was answered she came upon him like a storm. Stock's face met Tilly's churning breasts head-on as they began to break like waves upon the bows of his cheeks, her ferocious back-lit hair lashing the decks of his thinning scalp, until, like a storm at sea, she withdrew. Momentarily Stock's head held its position before plunging forward, his storm-swept forehead shattering his plate as it hit the table.

"What's a matter with him?" The water nymph had returned. She snapped the twenty-dollar bill into the taut darkness of her stocking top and watched as I poured the first of the San Badino *slightly sparkling* onto the plant that I had now identified as a *Dracaena fragrans*, *Dracaena fragrans moribunda* to give it its full name.

"He's fine," I said. "He likes his food." Unwilling to be sidetracked by her concern for my comatose colleague, I stepped up to the coat check and presented my token. On the fifth attempt the attendant succeeded in hoisting the seventy-litre sack of compost onto the counter. I dropped a quarter into the gratuities saucer and dragged my reclaimed dirt back to where the ailing *Dracaena*, having drunk its fill, was now sitting in a pool of its own earthy piss.

I lay the soggy-footed plant on its side and gave its pot a series of hefty slaps. A fibrous whirlpool of spent dirt and wizened root fell onto the table top, its arachnoid tendrils sucking on the ball of starved earth like a spider feeding on a long-dead fly. Doing my best not to damage the tiny filaments through which the plant had been drawing its scant sustenance, I teased the starving roots away from the pathetic little earth ball and with a butter knife cut back some of the longer outgrowths.

Another dancer had taken over from the snake-eyed Tilly. I recognised her. It was Hedda Foremen. She was hanging from a pole, looking out through the obscene bifurcation formed by her raised and parted legs, as though through the sights of some huge gun. With a shudder I remembered the three hundred bucks I'd offered her to come back to my hotel two nights before. Pondering the frankness of her refusal and the cleft in her pants, I picked up the corkscrew and used it to bore a hole in the bottom of the champagne bucket. No one was watching. Their priapic virilia safely fastened beneath their zipper trelliswork, the pot-bound punters were ogling Hedda. By the time she'd slithered down from her pole, I was already sweeping the fragments of broken crockery from around Stock's face into my newly bored planter. For once, as Hedda's powerful thighs began their advance across the dance floor, I wasn't paying attention. I was crouched over the open bag of compost. With an empty champagne glass I was scooping dollops of black soil onto the drainage material so conveniently provided by Stock's broken plate. Then, easing

the palm's roots once more out of their foetal cringe, I
placed them in the pot and began draping them in a velvet
cloak of black compost. When only the palm's leaves could
be seen, I patted the compost down and gave the plant a
thorough soaking with the second bottle of San Badino.
Almost immediately a carbonated slurry began draining
from the bucket towards the edge of the table where
Hedda's buttocks, recently arrived, were waiting to touch
down next to Stock's catatonic countenance. When I looked
up it was just in time to see her chiffon-clad cheeks
damming the course of the dirty brook. Hedda looked
round, aware that her concentration had been broken by the
unpleasant sensation of something cold and wet soaking
into her pants. Leaping up, she wheeled round and stood
glaring at me as her soiled underwear dripped into the
puddle that was forming on the floor. Instinctively I raised
my glass. It was filled with John Innes No. 2 Compost. My
gallant gesture was misinterpreted. "What is it with perverts
like you?" Other punters were craning forward now,
struggling to see the form of my particular perversity.
Seeing the dark puddle in which the furious dancer stood
screaming, someone in the crowd called out, "Hey, Hedda,
did you shit your pants?" His gallant remark did little to
calm the situation. With a roar Hedda turned on me.
Lunging across the table she knocked the glass from my

hand, and what she would have done next I will never know, for at that moment her stratospheric heels lost their balance. On the wet floor her lunge became a skitter. Her legs racing like a flicker book, she grabbed in desperation at the table's edge. Like the last moments of the *Titanic*, the table pitched upright: bottles, glasses, cellphones, Stock's head, all slid towards the cadent dancer. All except for the *Dracaena*. That I had saved, and through its variegated foliage I watched as another burst of strobe lighting rendered the final moments of Hedda's crash in slow motion. For an eternity she seemed to hang in the air, then the strobe cut out and she fell.

The upturned table had been enough to wake Stock from his coma. A fragment of broken crockery was still sticking to his forehead when he raised his face and saw Hedda. "I thought you said she didn't go down?" he said. The next thing I remember was the sound of doors opening, closing, the fresh air on my face, my arms held like handles by the two gorillas who replanted me on the street. Two heavy thuds as Stock and the near-full bag of compost were dumped alongside me. Where they are now I have no idea. The last I remember was flinging a fistful of bills into the driver's greasy hand as I stepped from a cab. In the back seat Stock was sleeping like a baby, his head nestled on a pillow of compost. He had the same look of contentment on his grubby face that he wore when Hedda's breasts enveloped him in their milky squall. If the money's not run out they're probably both still there. Turning in circles about the city. Those clubs are all the same, full of men who've forgotten how much they need their Mother Earth.

How to Prune the Rose
with Pablo Neruda

Tools:
Secateurs
Courage
Love

I have named you queen,
My sleeping one.
At winter's approach I have watched you grow drowsy
Falling into a sleep that deepens
With each passing day.
While I, your summer lover
Who spent long afternoons
And late nights by your side,
Drinking in your perfume,
Am left behind.
When I approach you now, it is not with a kiss,
But with a blade in my hands.
Forgive me my love. You must,
For I am the guardian of our love.
Before I sleep I will cut away your deadwood,
Your damaged branches,
Your crossing and congested stems will I remove.
So that you will not wound yourself in the troubled
    dreams that come

When the north wind shakes your boughs.
Free flowing air will circulate among your stems
And no disease will trouble your rosy limbs.
Each cut is kind,
The blades close tight above the bud
Whose growth will make your figure fair
In summers yet to come.
I angle my secateurs upwards
With each diagonal cut an oval of fleshy white pith
    appears.
They hang about your body like moonstones.

How shocked I am at what I have done.
You stand, my love, barely a foot from the ground
Your leaves all gone now, clad only in a coat of thorns
With which you prick and scratch at me
And I feel myself alone once more.
And I too long for winter to wrap me in its cloak of ether
To sleep knowing, deep in my own white pith, that you
    will wake me in the spring.
With your first blood-red bloom you will summon me
    to your side
And our love will live again.

List of Illustrations